MW01491419

This breathtaking epic poem expands the heart beyond the small stories we tell about God and existence itself. Rooted in Latter-day Saint theology, it feels both familiar and profoundly new. It creates an exhilarating spaciousness for imagining what could be. Sharlee Mullins Glenn's vision speaks to a deep heart-knowing—gently healing the ache of Mother God's quiet absence and restoring the sense of her intimate and infinite love at work in our lives.

—Aubrey Chaves
co-host of the *Faith Matters* podcast

Sharlee Mullins Glenn's epic poem *Brighter and Brighter* is a masterpiece—epic in all the senses of the word. Like its Homeric and Miltonian predecessors, it pursues the relations between Gods and humans with delicious and well-wrought blank verse in iambic pentameter. Glenn uses the form to capture the depth and drama and power and meaning of one of our most treasured Latter-day Saint foundational stories. But here's the thing. It is so original. Creative. And draws on so many gorgeous ideas. She uses the poetic form with skill and adroit beauty—and the work opens new possibilities for theology by exploring the Divine Feminine with the depth and standing it deserves. She unlocks our canon to present meaningful female participation and gives them presence and voice—

creating a cast of women protagonists equal in power and influence with the male figures we know so well from other tellings. I also love the work for its exploring the creation with references to science, evolution, and even quantum mechanics, tying ancient concepts with modern sensibilities.

But let me offer a warning. I kept finding my eyes watering as I read. A lot. Keep tissues nearby. There is beauty in the language, insight in the way it unfolds new redemptive narratives about the Preexistence, the Creation, and the Fall. Glenn offers vibrant speculation and opens a revelatory enlargement to doctrines recognizing that there were other actors in these earth-veiled events.

Read this book. The form demands we read it out loud. Voice it together with friends and loved ones. Perform it in book groups. Read it around campfires with the youth. One thing I feel pretty certain about is that this will become a classic of our people's poetic theological narratives. In my mind, it already is.

—Steven L. Peck
biologist, poet, novelist;
author of *A Short Stay in Hell,*
Evolving Faith, Heike's Void

A beautiful invitation to see something very old in a very new way. This story invites us into new layers of thought, of words, of completion. Bringing the Mother back into the Motherless House of this world is a powerful contribution. Thank you, Sharlee, for accepting the call to be a visionary.

—Carol Lynn Pearson
author of *Finding Mother God*
and *Mother Wove the Morning*

What were women doing during the great premortal council in heaven? Did Eve have another name before her birth and after her death, the way Adam is also Michael? Sharlee Mullins Glenn sees these gaps in scripture, and approaches God with the offering of her own religious imagination. In the rhythmic flow of poetry, she finds a space to search for her foremothers. We may not have answers to Sharlee's questions, but she gives us the gift of a holy wonder about how things might have been—and in questions of faith, sometimes that wonder is enough.

—James Goldberg
author of *Let Me Drown with Moses*
and *Tales of the Chelm First Ward*

Sharlee Mullins Glenn has re-imagined the plan of salvation in fascinating ways. I deeply appreciate the expansive consideration of how our Mother in Heaven could have reigned with such luminous love. Read on!

—McArthur Krishna
author of the *Girls's* and *Boys's Guide
to Heavenly Mother*, *Cherish*, and
Study Guide to Heavenly Mother

Sharlee Mullins Glenn's new epic poem *Brighter and Brighter until the Perfect Day* is an important new addition to the body of Latter-day Saint literature. The story of creation is told in blank verse that almost compels the reader to keep reading. The account's originality and depth also engage the reader profoundly. The characters are complex and interesting, and have names. There are also surprises that I will leave readers to learn for themselves in their own reading. I will have this book in my library as soon as it is published.

—Susan Elizabeth Howe
retired BYU English Professor,
author of *Infinite Disguises*,
former editor of *Exponent II*,
former poetry editor of *Dialogue*,
recipient of the AML Lifetime Achievement Award

Sharlee Mullins Glenn's epic poem is an ambitious and beautiful rendering of Latter-day Saint beliefs and yearnings regarding the feminine divine, the ethos of existence, and the centrality of agency, relationships, and love."

—Fiona Givens
co-author of *The God Who Weeps*,
The Crucible of Doubt, *The Christ Who Heals*,
and *All Things New*

Brighter
AND Brighter
until the
Perfect Day

BCC PRESS

BY COMMON CONSENT PRESS is a non-profit publisher dedicated to producing affordable, high-quality books that help define and shape the Latter-day Saint experience. BCC Press publishes books that address all aspects of Mormon life. Our mission includes finding manuscripts that will contribute to the lives of thoughtful Latter-day Saints, mentoring authors and nurturing projects to completion, and distributing important books to the Mormon audience at the lowest possible cost.

FOREWORD BY MICHAEL AUSTIN

Brighter AND Brighter until the Perfect Day

Sharlee Mullins Glenn

For information contact
By Common Consent Press
972 East Burnham Lane
Draper, Utah 84020

Cover art: "Creator Goddess" by J. Kirk Richards
Cover design: D Christian Harrison
Illustrations: Sara Forbush
Book design: Andrew Heiss

www.bccpress.org
ISBN-13: 978-1-961471-20-7

10 9 8 7 6 5 4 3 2 1

*For Devin, whose love of
epic poetry, reverence for the
feminine divine, and unwarranted
but unwavering faith in my abilities
gave me both the motivation and the
confidence to undertake such
a preposterous endeavor.*

FOREWORD

Michael Austin

When Orson F. Whitney prophesied in 1888 that Latter-day Saints would "yet have Miltons and Shakespeares of our own," he was, among other things, making a claim about poetic form. Perhaps more than any other general authority of his day, Whitney saw Mormonism as a coherent set of beautiful ideas that could form the basis of significant literature. What could be more significant than William Shakespeare's moving tragedies or John Milton's magnificent Christian Epic, *Paradise Lost?* Whitney never tried his hand at Shakespearean drama. But in 1904, he did publish his lengthy epic poem, *Elias*, which told the histories of the Old Testament, the New Testament, the Book of Mormon, and the early Latter-day Saint movement in ten cantos. Never one for half measures, Whitney included cantos in Miltonic blank verse, Spenserian Stanzas, closed heroic couplets, and English ballad stanzas.

As a series of discrete poems, *Elias* has many high points. Whitney has a good command of poetic diction, and his language sometimes soars. As a classical epic, though, it falls flat because it tries to tell too many stories in too many ways without an overarching theme or character. Rather than serving as a focal point for the stories, the figure of Elias becomes a scriptural Forrest Gump who makes appearances throughout sacred history without ever really adding much to the story.

Since Whitney, nearly a dozen Latter-day Saint poets have attempted to cast some part of their religious story in an epic form. Some have used the plot of the Book of Mormon as epic material, and others have used the founding of the Church and trek across the plains. But 150 years after Whitney's famous prediction, we are still waiting for our Milton to appear.

But the wait may well be over.

Sharlee Mullins Glenn, with her remarkable new epic *Brighter and Brighter until the Perfect Day*, comes closer than any poet ever has to being a "Milton of our own." Her poem tells roughly the same story that *Paradise Lost* tells—the rebellion of Satan and the Fall of Adam and Eve. But it tells this story as only one steeped in a Latter-day Saint worldview can. Everything that, for Milton, occurred among angels and devils before the creation of humanity is set in a common pre-existence, where Jesus, Lucifer, and all of us lived in a state of innocence and inexperience.

Glenn presents God's plan, Satan's plan, and the War in Heaven as discussions that involved every human soul that has ever existed. And she presents the Fall, when it occurs, as an indispensable part of that plan. For Christians of Milton's time, these would have been unthinkable heresies. For Latter-day Saints, they are part of a coherent worldview that sees God, Christ, Satan, and all of humanity as manifestations of the same kind of being, separated only by degree and by the consequences of their choices.

Glenn also restores to its proper place the Latter-day Saint doctrine of the feminine divine—a Mother-in-Heaven who joins with a Father-in-Heaven to govern all of creation with a unity of affection and purpose. The result is a decisive recentering of the feminine divine into the Latter-day Saint version of the creation story. This recentering is crucial. From Milton on, the feminine presence has been absent in the Christian creation story, except for the character of Eve, who usually gets the blame for the Fall. In *Brighter and Brighter until the Perfect Day*, the Divine Mother is in the story from the beginning, and other pre-existent women play major roles—including

Eve, whose heroic choice makes it possible for humans to progress. But there is no anti-male bias here, either. For Glenn, men and women work together in equal partnership to create the world and bring salvation to all of humankind.

Sharlee Mullins Glenn does all of this in gorgeous blank verse that often approaches the language of Milton himself. But nothing about this poem is mimicry. Glenn understands Milton and the epic tradition on a deep level, and *Brighter and Brighter until the Perfect Day* succeeds by doing for the Latter-day Saint tradition what Dante did for Catholicism and Milton did for dissenting Protestantism. Glenn starts with the perspective that LDS doctrine has both coherence and intellectual weight, and then uses that doctrine to create a thing of beauty.

PREFACE

Sharlee Mullins Glenn

Brighter and Brighter until the Perfect Day is an epic poem, written, like Milton's *Paradise Lost*, in English blank verse, or unrhymed iambic pentameter. Few people write epic poems anymore, and I doubt that many people read them. Writer and critic Clive James argues, though, that there will always be epic poems "because every human life contains one."[1]

I felt compelled to use the challenging form of the epic poem to explore some of the big existential ideas I have

---

1. Clive James, "Clive James on His New Epic Poem: 'The Story of a Mind Heading into Oblivion,'" *The Guardian*, September 1, 2018, https://www.theguardian.com/books/2018/sep/01/clive-james-poem-story-mind-heading-obivion.

wrestled with for many years. It seemed the only appropriate structure for what I was trying to do. As Stephen Sondheim so famously observed, content does sometimes dictate form.[2]

As with all epic poems, this one is best experienced when read or heard aloud.

Though based on Latter-day Saint doctrine, *Brighter and Brighter* is a work of fiction and is speculative in nature. It is a literary experiment of sorts, written for the purpose of creative excogitation. In writing the poem, my aim was to create a framework that could accommodate both revealed doctrine and reasoned speculation.

Brighter and Brighter does endeavor to bring together various doctrines concerning the nature of God, the centrality and inviolability of agency, the reality of the feminine divine, the preeminence of love, and revealed truths about intelligence, light, and matter into one coherent whole. In this sense, it is at least a partial attempt at a rational theology, which James Faulconer defines as "explaining what we believe by giving it a rational structure."[3]

---

2.   Stephen Sondheim, *Finishing the Hat: Collected Lyrics (1954–1981) with Attendant Comments, Principles, Heresies, Grudges, Whines and Anecdotes* (New York, NY: Alfred A. Knopf, 2011).

3.   James E. Faulconer, *Faith, Philosophy, Scripture* (Provo, Utah: Neal A. Maxwell Institute for Religious Scholarship, Brigham Young University, 2010), p. 59.

But in the end, *Brighter and Brighter* is fiction. One early reader of the manuscript asked why I believe the Holy Ghost is Heavenly Mother. I responded that I don't. Or, at least, I don't know for sure (though it does make sense to me on many levels, and though there is evidence, both textual and archeological, that would point to this conclusion). Still, it's speculation, not doctrine. Reasoned speculation, though, is vital to examining one's *weltanschauung* and expanding one's capacity for creative and generative thinking. This is what I'm hoping to accomplish with *Brighter and Brighter*. I want readers to consider many different possibilities, not only in relation to Heavenly Mother, but also the Creation, the Fall, the purposes of mortality, the nature of progression, and so on. Herein lies the beauty of fiction. I am not attempting to set forth doctrine; merely using imagination to present interesting (and feasible) new perspectives. Fundamentally, that is what *Brighter and Brighter* is—an offering of imagination.

My hope is that my poem might engage you, the reader, in a worthwhile literary experience while prompting you to think deeply about existential and theological questions, more closely examine the boundaries of your own paradigms, and consider fresh new possibilities.

—DOCTRINE & COVENANTS 50:24

In time long past, before the world was formed,
the hosts of heaven, dressed in robes of light,
convened beneath the highest airy peak
that towered over Kolob's misty plains,
a boundless span of shimmering points of light
as far as eye could see, and then beyond.

And in their midst, a fellowship of beings
who shone most brightly with the light of truth—
the great and noble of the heavenly hosts.
Among these were Jehovah, firstborn Son;
and gracious Ora, daughter of the light;
and Lucifer, the shining morning star;
and faithful Michael; brave Adira too,
and Nava, Ezrah, Abigail, and more.

Then in a blaze of radiance unsurpassed
the great and glorious Elohim appeared,
not spirits sole, but bodies glorified,
unmatched in luminescence and in grace.
Their visages aglow with warming love,
They looked upon Their children in delight.
"The time is here!" They spoke as one, though two.
"Beloved heirs, we've taught you all we can
within this realm of unembodied forms.
You've learned, progressed, and grown in truth and light.
Intelligence must now with matter join
that you, along this journey, may proceed
toward Eternal Life and crowning joy."

The hosts of heaven cheered in jubilee.

"The plan is this." Their Parents' words rang clear.
"We will create a world for you to share—
a place where spirits will be clothed in flesh,
where you may taste the bitter and the sweet
and feel both pain and pleasure, joy and grief.
A place where opposition will abound
where you must choose and through your choices learn
to seek the light, to love, forgive, and serve."

Pure wonder filled the hearts of those who heard.
Their Mother smiled, and love blazed from Her eyes.
"The plan is that you make your way back home."

Then Father spoke. "It will be hard," He said.
"There will be pain and anguish, death and grief—
a shadowed path of sorrow and of strife.
And know this truth: we cannot walk with you.
A veil will fall, obscuring all you've known,
for you, by faith's dim light, must make your way."

The children stirred, their voices murm'ring low.
"But how?" one asked, his voice betraying fear.
"We're sure to stumble, falter, fail, misjudge . . ."

"In fact, you will," the Father said. "No doubt.
"Indeed, that is the point. For only as
you stumble will you learn, and only as
you reap the certain harvest of your choices
will discernment grow. You will make mistakes—
for one must practice to become a god."

"But when we choose amiss, our light recedes,"
said one whose earnest countenance shone fair.

"It's true," the Mother said. "And that is why
we will provide a Savior for you all,

a hybrid soul, half mortal, half divine,
a being whose light and glory are so bright
that He can do what no one else can do—
abstain from sin and live a faultless life.
This means that He, for you, can bear the cost
exacted by this universe of laws
for all who take upon themselves His name
and turn to Him to be redeemed and healed.
As oft as you will turn, you'll be restored
and grow from grace to grace, receiving light."

The Mother paused; then anguish filled Her voice.
"This is a task of overwhelming weight
requiring sacrifice too great to frame.
It is too much to ask of anyone
and must be offered up without duress."

Deep silence settled over all the sphere.
All turned to gaze at the Beloved Son
who moved toward the mighty Elohim
resplendent in His dazzling robes of fire,
more luminous by far than all the hosts
of spirit children in that realm of light.

His words were simple—meek and sure at once:
"Here am I. Send me. My will is thine."

Great Elohim embraced Their cherished son,
Their eyes aglow with pride but also grief.
There is no heavier load to bear than this—
the knowledge that your child must suffer pain.
And this would be no ordinary pain,
but all the anguish of a wounded world.

Then Elohim turned to the gathered hosts
with arms outstretched toward the Holy One.
"Behold your Savior, our Beloved Son."

A billion lights shone out in adoration.
A billion souls broke forth in songs of praise.

"Jehovah, the anointed one," said El.
"Christ, Jesus; great Redeemer of the world."

Again, the hosts of heaven cried with joy.

But one there was whose heart grew dark with greed—
Proud Lucifer, known as the Morning Star.
He was in brightness next unto Jehovah.
Why, then, should he not be the Chosen One?
For eons, he had been o'ershadowed by
the prized Jehovah, the Beloved Son.

The Mother then addressed the waiting throngs:
"All those who follow Christ will be redeemed.
The choice is yours; the power lies with you.
We will not, cannot, override your will."

The Morning Star sensed muted hesitance
begin to grow in hearts of certain there.
He seized his chance and, waiting not, stepped forth
and deftly raised his voice for all to hear.

"Dear siblings," he began in dulcet tones.
"This plan is fraught with peril and with risk.
With stakes so high, you cannot chance defeat.
Hear now my own proposal for your course:

Entrust *me* with your light and will—that light
which you have gained through diligence and care
through all these many stages of our being.
Give me that glory now (no, do not fear—
I will restore it yet again to you),
for with that glory (and with your free will)
I can secure for you safe passage through
the world of matter, unrefined and thorny.
I will ensure that you will act aright
in every case, for you will have no choice.
And thus, you will be spared the consequence
of sin and come again, unblemished, here."

A rumbling murmur spread throughout the throng.
The eyes of most turned back to Elohim,
but some eyes lingered on the Morning Star,
uneasy, hopeful, hesitant, unsure.

Then Elah spoke, Her voice with sorrow rife.
"Oh, Lucifer, my son, it's not too late
to turn away from this ignoble path.
You are belov'd, a son of boundless gifts.
We long to share all that we have with you,
but you must not subvert the hallowed plan;
for, as you know, free will is paramount,
for without freedom there can be no growth,
no good, no joy, no love, no exaltation."

Proud Lucifer felt spite descend like fog
and spread throughout his heart like poisoned sludge.
He sensed the eyes of legions fixed on him
as hubris and compunction in him clashed,
then heard a whispered wheedling from behind:
"You speak aright, and many here will trust
and pledge to you our loyalty and oath.
Why should the Morning Star be thus disgraced
while prized Jehovah once again prevails?"

These words snaked through his ears—oh, sweet
    seduction!—
'til pride and lust for power him overwhelmed.
This was his kairos, his defining moment,
he knew that there would be no turning back.
He wavered but a breath, and then rose taller
and, turning to the throng of spirits, cried:
"Choose me! And I will promise your return.
Choose him, and risk destruction, pain, and death!"

His words hung in the air like noxious mist.
Then, rising in a blaze of crimson flame,
he threw one venomed glance toward Jehovah,
and, trailing sparks of lightning, took his leave.
Some followed, resolute, and some uncertain,
some casting eyes about them as they went.
But most turned back, their eyes fixed on Jehovah.

A cloud of silence fell upon the throng.
Then from the midst spoke one of earnest heart:
"Dear Mother, Father, Savior of the world,
please know that we will hearken to Thy word—
and yet we feel a deep and rightful fear.
How can we find our way through darkened paths
without the light your presence e'er supplies?"

Jehovah looked with mercy at the crowd,
then turning to address His Parents said:
"If this would not disrupt the crucial plan,
a portion of my light I would bestow
on each of these, my sisters and my brothers,
a spark of luminescence for their soul."

Great El and Elah smiled in approbation,
then, turning to the concourse, thus proclaimed:
"A portion of the light of Christ you'll bring
when, to the earth you'll go to take on flesh—
your first endowment in the mortal world."

"And there is more," said Elah soothingly.
"For other beacons bright we will provide
to act as lodestars as you make your way.
Wise prophets from among you we will call—
good men and women full of light and truth,
whose gifts of vision and of prophecy
empower them to hear, and see, and lead.
These seers we will appoint to be your guides
in every generation on the earth.

But though these prophets will be foreordained
to witness of your Savior and reveal
some portion of the light that you'll require

to grow in love and power, grace by grace,
they will be human too, bound by their time.
Though seers they are, they'll also mortals be,
sent on this journey, just as you, to grow.
Thus, you must keep your focus firmly set
upon the solid Rock of your Salvation,
on Christ, the Lord, the Way, the Truth, the Life.
For you will agents be unto yourselves
with pow'r to seek, to choose, to gather light,
then shine that light that others too may see."

"It's all about this vital light," said El.
"The light you bear, the light you gain, the light
you share." He paused, then, smiling, looked around.
"The hoped-for aim is that you all become
pure conduits of light—receiving light,
bequeathing light in one continuous flow.
For this is truth eternal, that the more
you give, the greater your capacity
to reap, to grow, to learn, and to obtain."

The hosts of heav'n sang out with joyful voice:

O light resplendent, light divine
Which shineth forth from God's own face
Same light which giveth sight to eye
And lendeth life, and filleth space.

Light is the law that governs all
That quickens mind and truth affirms
Such light and truth, God's glory make
And, to our hearts, God's grace confirms.

O God, may we receive Thy light
'Til filled to brim we overflow
Ablaze with love, alight with joy
And draw all friends into its glow.

Illume our minds, enlarge our hearts
Beam out thy blaze into our souls
That we, like Thee, be filled with light
And stand before thee—radiant, whole.

"Remember, too, that you'll not be alone,"
 said Elah, and Her smile was warm with care.
"For you will not be solitary beings
 but, rather, will belong to close-knit clans
 joined by birth and bound through generations.
 And you will share relationship divine
 with *every* child of ours upon the earth.
 Your charge will be to help and serve and lift
 as one expansive unit bound by love
 and sealed in holy consanguinity."

"This sealing is imperative," said El.
"For we must set you free for you to grow
 and cannot force you back against your will.
 You must return of your own free accord
 and join yourselves again, embodied souls,
 to us and to each other and to Christ
 through covenants divine in holy shrines
 made binding through the rites of godly pow'r.
 For by this power, we are knit as one
 through quantum intertwining; nevermore
 to be detached, estranged, or drawn apart."

"Herein is much for you to comprehend,"
 said Elah, in a tone of purest love.
"And there is still more wisdom to impart.
 But know this now: you will not walk alone.
 Please take some time to contemplate these points,
 then we'll return with further light and truth."

The hosts of heaven milled about, amazed
 by all they'd heard. Some gathered in small groups
 to share their thoughts aloud, while others sought
 a private space to ponder on their own.
 The larger part converged upon Jehovah,
 replete with gratitude and joyful hearts.
 He spoke to each in turn with sweet concern,

then graciously withdrew to take His rest.
Bright Ora found Him in His favored place.
He welcomed her within his warm embrace.
"Dear sister, are you troubled?" asked Jehovah.
"You know me well, dear brother," she replied.
"I'm fearful now that Lucifer has fled.
You know as well as I that he will not
retract his words, back down, or change his course.
His pride is such that it will drive him on,
relentless, fierce, unyielding, to the end.
We've watched this burgeoning within his soul—
this thirst for honor, veneration, pow'r.
You saw his light turn dark; within his heart
he's given place for evil to expand.
He will not rest until our Parents' plan
he's thwarted and persuaded all he can
to follow him. He wants to be their god."

"I sense you're right, dear sister," said Jehovah.
"But we must trust the wisdom of the plan,
and in the strength and faith of all the heirs."
"Indeed," said she. "And yet, I wonder still
if there is more that we can yet bestow
to strengthen all God's children on the earth.
As souls embodied, Elohim cannot
walk with Their children while they're on the earth.

The Plan requires this sacred separation.
But you and I, as spirits, can attend
and offer light and guidance—comfort too—
and witness of our Parents and of truth,
until that time when you must take on flesh
and, this, in the meridian of time,
that you may be the Savior of the world.
And once you conquer death and rise again,
exalted, you must take your rightful place,
to sit at God's own side in heav'nly courts,
and reign in righteousness throughout all time.

But what if—as a spirit—I remain
and choose to wait to clothe myself in flesh
'til every other spirit has been born?
Then I, unbound by body, could abide
and act as witness, comforter, and guide."

A sudden stillness settled 'round the pair.
Jehovah's face grew tender, full of awe.
"I'm not surprised at all that you would choose
to make this selfless sacrifice," He said.
"For you a bearer of the light could be,
transmitting beams from Elohim's own throne.
As spirit, you would not be circumscribed
by time or space, but omnipresent be."

But then a shadow passed across His face.
"But are you truly willing to be last?
The very last? For every other spirit
will obtain that body which we all
aspire to gain, while you discarnate will
remain until the mortal work is done."

"My mind is firm" said Ora with a nod.
"My sacrifice is no more hard to bear
than yours. Indeed, I could not do what you
must do, which you alone can bring to pass."

"You would not suffer mortal pain, it's true,"
said He. "But you would be anonymous;
a presence ever felt, but never seen."

"It's as I wish," said Ora, without pause.
"For just as you, I do not seek the praise,
but, rather, give the glory unto God
and only hope to buttress humankind."

Then Ora brought her plan before the Throne,
and Elohim received it with deep awe.
"Dear Ora, cherished daughter of the light,
your readiness to offer up yourself
imbues our hearts with wonder and esteem.
Because of this greathearted willingness,

thus offered without thought of recompense,
how great shall be your glory through all time,
and unto you is given now to know
your own portentous mission, foreordained."

The Mother took Her child in Her embrace.
"Your powers of perception are acute,
and wisdom, light, and truth glow in your being.
You have discerned that part which next we'll share:
A disembodied spirit is required
to move upon the earth which we shall form
bound not by mortal time nor space, but free
to be in the Eternal Now— and in
and through all things, creation's breath and source.
But I, not you, must take upon myself
this role, for as a Mother I cannot
do less; to you is giv'n a different charge."

Bright Ora, daughter of the light, was still.
"But, Mother, how is this to be? You are
a soul embodied—glorified and real."

"Let's summon dear Jehovah to us now,"
said El, and Elah nodded Her assent.
When He had come, Their Parents drew them near.

"Dear Son and Daughter, hear these needful words:
That all our children may be gathered in,
a paired redemption must be set in place.
Jehovah, spirit, must a body take
that He may lay it down again for all,
then take it up, renewed, when death is won.
The Mother, soul embodied, glorified,
will lay Her body down for but a time
that She might with Her children be to guide,
to comfort, witness, and to sanctify."

Both Son and Daughter turned to Mother God,
emotion swelling deep within their hearts.
"I see that this must be," the Daughter said.
"For this is work that only you can do.
To set aside that prize that we all seek,
your wondrous body, infinite and pure,
that you may be with us while on the earth.
It is a gift of overwhelming worth."

Then Mother, Father, Daughter, Son embraced,
united in Their gratitude and aim.

"But what is my part in this hallowed plan?"
asked Ora, and her earnestness was clear.

As Elah looked upon Her eager child,
a cloud of deepest sadness crossed Her face.
"For many generations, humankind
will know of both their Parents and Their love—
both male and female, joined in holy union,
thus bringing poise and balance into life.
The Mother shall be known by many names—
Shaddai, the Holy Spirit, Asherah,
the Lady Wisdom, Mother Tree, and more.
But then the time will come when frightened men
will exile Lady Wisdom. They'll remove
me from the temple and forbid my name
be spoken, and expunge but vaguest hints
from worship and their books of holy writ.
From that time on, I'll mostly be forgot.
But then will come the final dispensation,
a time of open hearts and restoration.
I'll slowly start to be unveiled again.
Thus, line by line, and glimpse by shaded glimpse,
my presence and my pow'r will be revealed
until that time when I'll be ushered back
and to the holy temple be restored,
thus heralded by one so foreordained—
a mighty prophetess who will proclaim
the doctrine of the Mother God Divine.
And then our children will be taught again

the truth of Heaven'ly Parents that the earth
be equalized and wholeness be restored."

Here Elah paused, and smiled upon Her child.
"That prophetess, my treasured one, is you."

And when the hosts of heav'n again convened,
there once again rang out a shout of joy
as Father God explained the Mother's gift:

"On earth, She shall be called the Holy Ghost,
and shall be Comforter and faithful guide.
As spirit, She, to spirit, can transmit
the light and knowledge needed for this quest,
and will bear witness of all truth received.
But She will have an even weightier role
as purifier of each blemished being,
for each of you will act amiss at times,
and some will yield to evil's wanton sway,
inflicting harm and wounding both themselves
and others too in ways unthinkable
and cruel, resulting in a loss of light.
Because of Christ's atoning sacrifice,
you can repent and be forgiven as
you turn to Him in faith and take His name.
But to the Holy Spirit will be giv'n
the power to restore your injured souls."

The hosts cried out in songs of highest praise,
and then one spake the question of her heart:
"But Mother, if our eyes cannot discern
Your Spirit's form, and if all mem'ry will
be blotted out, then how will you be known?"

The Mother stood majestic—fie'ry love,
and blazing warmth, and brilliant flaming pow'r.
"My children, you will see me in the clouds,
in fire, and sunrise, and the brooding dove.
You'll hear me in the cry of newborn babes,
the sweet and hushful whisper of the breeze.
You'll find me in the tops of ancient peaks,
in whirlwinds and hot pillars of pure light,
in wombs, and tombs, and slender blades of grass."

The hosts fell to their knees in wonderment
at all that Elah would forego for them.

With all the vital pieces now in place,
the work of the creation could begin.
The great and noble sat in council with
the mighty Elohim to undertake
the final preparations of the plan.

"Since our beloved Son, the sacred Word,
will bring about the work of your salvation,

He will create the earth, the skies, the seas
by our own pow'r and under our direction.
You, too, will help in this important work,
and foreordained will be for certain roles
according to the gifts you have refined."

The Heavenly Parents looked with love upon
Their valiant spirit children gathered there.

"Adira, you are fearless, wise, and strong;
your powers of discernment are unmatched.
Good Michael, you have proved that you will be
obedient, faithful, constant, ever true.
You two will be the first of sapient beings.
On earth you shall be known as Eve and Adam,
and yours will be the charge to teach your young
to walk uprightly and good stewards be."

Adira and good Michael bowed their heads,
then with resolve, they signaled their accord.

"And now, for an appointment of great weight:
the mortal mother of our treasured Son
must be a vessel of the purest light
for unto her will fall the stewardship
of raising Him who is the Son of God.

Dear Nava, if to this you will agree,
you will be mother to our cherished boy.
To you the Holy Spirit will convey
the seed of El, for half divine the child
must be to have the pow'r to overcome
the world and triumph over death and sin.
Your name while on the earth shall Mary be
and though you will be born of lowly station,
henceforth, will every creature call you blessed."

Fair Nava knelt in humble acquiescence.
"The handmaid of my Parents I will be."

"Our gratitude for you is without end,"
said Elah, as deep sorrow filled her eyes.
"For you, like us, will sacrifice your son.
A steady, brave companion you will need
who can assist you in this pond'rous task
and who, withholding nothing, will commit
to helping raise the Savior of the World.
Good Ezrah, we cannot conceive another
as fit as you to undertake this charge."

Without the slightest hint of hesitation
good Ezrah rose and took fair Nava's hand.

"Now, Ora, treasured daughter of the light,
to you is giv'n a work of great import,
for you will speak with power and with might—
a prophetess of courage you will be
in once again revealing Mother God
that balance be restored and nature healed."

Then others, too, were given their commission,
to each according to the light they bore.

And now the time had come to form the earth
and every living thing which would abide
upon the land and in the air and sea,
in spirit first, and then in temporal form.

Great Elohim o'ersaw this mighty work
accomplished by the Word, Their Firstborn Son.

The Gods surveyed the vast expanse of space
and there saw matter to be organized
into a world befitting humankind.
"Let form and function be forever joined
in this, the workmanship of our own hands!"

"First, into shadow we will send the light
by our own Word," said El. "Let there be light."
And there was light. And then They formed the earth,

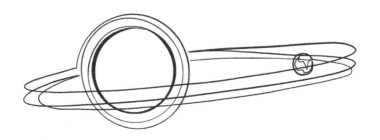

a perfect sphere, to orbit 'round the sun
(the source of light and warmth and cosmic pull)
while turning, turning, turning on its shaft,
thus forming first the day and then the night
and then again, in one eternal round.

And thus advanced the handiwork of God
by virtue of the Spirit through the Word.
The council worked in rapturous delight,
first weaving sky, then sculpting land and sea.
And at the end of each creative phase
they were content, and God declared it good.

They set in motion all the heav'nly orbs
with light to rule the day and also night
that, whether light direct or light reflected,
no child would ever be without its glow.

At last, the earth was ready for new life.
From microbes, over eons, there evolved
new complex cells: porifera and coral,
crustaceans, fish, and ferns, and tetrapods,
then beetles, seed plants, conifers, and pines,
and turtles, star fish, bees, and ants, and deer,
and, finally, Homo Habilis. And then—

succeeding many more millenia
of change—a hominid sufficiently
evolved, with brain to reason and to choose.

The work was done, the graceful system set—
a brilliant, self-sustaining, constant round.

But meanwhile Lucifer, the Morning Star,
consumed with greed and galvanized by pride,
was ceaseless in his efforts to seduce
and lure away more spirits with his lies.
Esurient for power, he used fear
to prey upon the weaknesses of some
(a bargain struck: your light for your salvation)
while others he enticed with hollow vows,
false promises of title, station, rank.

And so, in his perversion of the truth,
he seized the light of those who followed him,
thus binding them to him with silken chains,
augmenting his own power with his spoils.
But since that pow'r was stolen, it was dark—
corrupted, twisted, warped, devoid of grace,
the inverse of the virtuous, holy force
that flowed like healing waters through all space—
a counterfeit of godly priesthood power.

And Satan saw the world that was created
and wanted to obtain it for himself,
desiring to be god of all the earth.
So, seeking to exalt himself, he led
his loyalists above the height of clouds
to claim the throne of the Almighty God.

Great Elohim yet pleaded for Their son
to turn his heart again toward the light,
but he had yielded to his lust for pow'r.
So there ensued a monumental battle
between the powers of darkness and of light.
But evil was no match for radiant good
and wickedness was vanquished by its might.

And thus, by his own actions, Satan fell.
Because of his rebellion and revolt,
he could no longer bear the brilliant blaze
of God's own presence or of Kolob's reach,
and so, he fell away and back and downward,
thence banished by his pride and blackened heart.
And all his servile vassals toppled with him,
recoiling from the beams of dazzling light
that blazed in righteous glory from above.

And all around the hosts of heaven wept.

Down, down, away from realms celestial,
away from hope of glory through God's plan,
for with no body, there could be no fullness.

But Satan's lust was undiminished still.
"Come, follow me! Upon the earth we'll dwell
and there we'll rule with power and with might."
And so, as specters to the earth they flew
to take their place as lords of all creation.

"You must know this," said Satan to his hosts.
"As spirits unembodied we exist
within a realm obscured from mortal eyes,
but can by other means exert our sway.
And bear in mind that we'll have the advantage
o'er all the other spirits who will come,
for once they venture through the mortal veil,
all mem'ry of Before will disappear.
And in due course, their bodies we will take.
Then they, not us, will be forever damned!"

Then, in the realms above, the council gathered,
and Elohim announced the joyous news:
At last, on earth, a form sufficiently
evolved to think and exercise free will.
Because, by chance, it was a male, from him
They would extract a single human strand

of DNA to form a frame for Man—
a body for his spirit to indwell.
And then, from Adam, Elohim would take
the code to modify and fashion Eve
(replace the Y with duplicated X).

And thus was Adam formed upon the earth
and by the Mother's breath became a soul.

But first the Gods prepared a threshold realm—
a place for preparation and instruction,
a Garden, lush and green and undefiled,
a higher plane than was the 3-brane world.

Into this Garden, Elohim placed Man
and taught him to convey his thoughts with speech
(a wondrous symbol set of sounds called language),
inviting him to relish and delight
in all the bounty of the Garden's joys.

"Now tend it well, and keep with mindful care
each vine, each tree, and every living thing;
for as a sapient being, it falls to you
to safeguard all creation in its sphere.
Of all the seeds, the herbs, the fruits, partake
without restraint. Yet not the flesh of beasts,
for they, like you, are vessels of our breath.

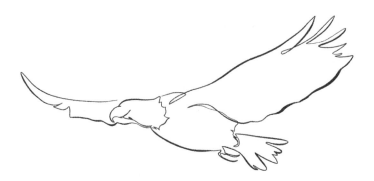

Partaking of their meat would introduce
brutality and bloodshed in this space
and would beget corruption, sin, and death.
So, heed our words, and walk with us in peace,
that you may dwell here long and talk with us,
as you prepare to rise and journey on.
But know, the choice is yours alone to make—
for we shall never bind you or constrain.
You have free will which we will not annul,
indeed, cannot, for it is elemental."

"Now, Adam, here's a joyful task for you:
Behold the beasts that roam the earth and air.
Please classify and catalogue them all.
Observe them, learn, and give to each a name
that you may know how best to care for them."

Then Adam swiftly set about this charge,
and as he named each creature one by one
his heart swelled wide with wonder, love, and awe.

One twilight, as he stroked the lion's mane,
Great Elohim drew near and stood in thought.
"Dear Adam, are you happy?" questioned El.
Good Adam thought a moment, then replied:
"I love this Garden and all creatures here.

I also love the time I spend with you.
But . . ." Here he paused, reluctant to go on.
"Speak freely, son," encouraged Mother God.
So, Adam spoke the sadness of his heart.
"I watch the beasts, how chimp communes with chimp,
and bear with bear, and hawk with hawk, and on.
And in my soul, I feel an empty space,
and long for a companion like myself,
as you and Father one another have."

Then Elah smiled, and radiance filled the Garden.
"We've waited long to hear you say those words.
A woman we will form—your equal match.
A partner true to whom you will be bound
throughout your time on earth and evermore."

"But this we could not do without assent
from you," continued El. "For it requires
that we take a fragment of your frame
that we may form a woman who will share
your nature, ethos, and capacity
to reason and distinguish good from ill.
For this, we need permission and consent."

"Oh, yes!" said Adam, eager to comply.

"Then we will cause a sleep to come on you,
and we'll remove a sample from your side—
a code of sorts from which we'll form a woman,
the soulmate that your spirit yearns to know."

So, Eve was formed and walked alongside Adam
in joy, and love, and mutual esteem.

Though they remembered nothing of Before,
they both increased in light and understanding
as with their loving Parents they conversed.

Then, Satan, knowing not the mind of God,
espied the Garden and was filled with wrath.
"The Gods have stolen my idea!" he raged.
"The concept of a perfect world was mine,
that no one would be lost. It was all mine!"

And meanwhile, Elohim prepared to leave,
whilst promising that They would soon return
with further light and knowledge for Their heirs,
allowing them to practice all they'd learned.

Then Satan, fallen angel, saw his chance.
And, hoping to upend God's gracious plan,
he entered quick into the verdant Garden
and took possession of the serpent's frame.

He found the woman playing with a lamb,
 and, feigning friendship, sidled close and said:
"This Garden overflows with lush delights;
 no end to all the treasures ripe to taste.
 Have you yet feasted on the stag, the quail, the lamb?"

With widened eyes, the woman studied him.
"Of all the fruit of all the plants you see,
 we freely may partake. But not the flesh
 of bird or beast, for so commanded God."

"But that is most desirable of all,"
 the serpent said. "Delicious to the taste."

"Why would we eat the flesh of living souls?"
 responded Eve, her hand upon the lamb.
"With them we share a bond. And if we did,
 as we've been told, then we would surely die."

"You will not die," the cunning serpent said.
"Instead, your eyes will see. You will be wise
 and better able, then, to care for these,
 your friends, and all of Gods' creations."

"I cannot, will not, disobey," said Eve.

"But, don't you see?" the scheming serpent said.
"You have free will; the Gods *want* you to choose.
It's why They left. Now, hurry; don't delay.
For if you eat, then you will move beyond
this interim and temporary space
and take your rightful place within the world
the Gods created for your propagation.
It's time for you to see the *truthful* world.
While here, you're safe, but wisdom will elude,
for without opposition, there can be
no growth, no knowledge, no enduring joy."

"And is there not another way?" asked Eve.

The Father of all Lies did not delay:
"There is no other way," responded he.

A sudden rush of wind swirled 'round the Tree
that flowered in the center of the Garden.

Eve paused, and then with courage unsurpassed,
the Mother of all Living made her choice.
"Then I will eat, that God's plan may advance."

But she was not prepared for what came next.
The serpent's deadly strike was swift and sure.

One sharp, bewildered cry, and then the fact
of lifeless form where once a living lamb.

"Now, you can eat, and it will feel no pain,"
the serpent said to Eve, who sat in shock,
eyes wide and welling, comprehending not
the spot of crimson seeping like a stain
across the milky fleece of quiet lamb.

Then, with the razored talon of the serpent,
Sly Satan slashed a chunk of fleshy meat
and, with a flourish, offered it to Eve.
"Now, do not fear," he said. "For you will soon
be wise." Eve hesitated for a beat,
then placed the tender morsel in her mouth.

"Just so!" said Satan, jubilant and smug.
"Now, go and get your Adam to partake."

With one last troubled glance at breathless lamb,
Eve found her way to Adam's favorite spot,
and saw him there attending to some ferns.

"Dear Adam, I have eaten of the fruit
that Elohim forbade you to partake.
I've made my choice and think that it was right

for now my eyes are open and I see
that we cannot progress unless we act
as agents for ourselves and claim the pow'r
that Elohim has given out of love.
To choose, there must a range of options be,
and we must be enticed. As innocents
in Eden, naive and unaware, we can't
do good because we know no other way.
But, knowing evil, we can *choose* the good;
and knowing darkness, we can *choose* the light.

Good Adam was distressed by what he heard.
"But, how can we our Parents disobey?"

"If we do not," said Eve. "Then we will not
progress beyond this place of innocence.
The evil serpent who beguiled me claimed
this was the only way. Now that my eyes
can see, I am not sure he spoke the truth.
But, still, because I have consumed the fruit—
the fruit which was proscribed—by the decree
of universal law, I cannot stay,
and you, dear Adam, will be left alone.
Again. Remember, too, that Elohim
commanded us to multiply and bear
good fruit, that in our seed we might have joy.

But this we cannot do if I must leave
and you remain alone here in the Garden."

Good Adam listened thoughtfully, then said:
"I see that this must be. Where is this fruit?
I will partake that humankind may be."

So, Adam ate, and something in him shifted.

The serpent, smirking, now approached the pair.
Their exile from the Garden drawing near
when, banished to the world, they'd surely fall
into his reach and be within his pow'r.

But then they heard the voices of the Gods.
In golden tones, great Elohim conversed.
"Quick!" Satan hissed. "You're naked; run and hide!"
And so, in shame, they hid themselves straightway.

"Adam. Eve. Where are you?" Elah called.

With downcast eyes, Their children inched to light
and stood before Them, awkward and restrained.

"Have you partaken of the flesh of beasts?"

"Yes," Adam said. "But I ate first," said Eve.
"The serpent did beguile me, and I ate."

El summoned Satan. "Show yourself forthwith."

Unable to defy, the serpent did.

"What are you doing here?" asked Mother God.

"I'm only doing what's been done before
in opening their eyes that they might see
and judge between the evil and the good.
It's what you said you wanted, was it not?"

"Oh, fallen Morning Star," grieved Father El.
"Since you have chosen darkness, you cannot
distinguish more the ways of light and grace,
but bring upon you misery and woe.
We know that your intent was to subvert
the Plan and take possession of the frames
created here for Adam and for Eve.
And so, we must place enmity between
our own beloved mortal heirs and you.
It's true that you have pow'r to bruise their heels,
but, through Jehovah, they can crush your head."

The fallen angel seethed in indignation
and with a voice of thunder hurled his threats.
God Mother and God Father rose, majestic.
"Depart!" They said, and he could not but heed.

With Satan gone, the Gods turned to Their children
and pulled them close into a warm embrace.
"Since death and sin have entered in the Garden,
the repercussions, real, must now be faced.
The laws of nature cannot be denied,
and every choice brings with it consequences.
Because you chose to eat the fruit forbidden,
this prepar'tory chapter is cut short
and from our presence you will be disjoined.
By eating flesh, your natures are made carnal;
hence, in the Garden you cannot remain.
Because your fallen natures make you mortal,
disease and sickness now will be your lot,
and weeds and thistles will spring forth to vex,
while entropy will be the ruling law.
You will grow old, and weaken, and decay,
and life will seem egregiously unfair.
Free will is requisite for joy and growth,
but also opens up the prospect of
abuse, for many will choose wrongly and
inflict the fallout of their choices on
themselves and others too. There will be war.
The powerful will prey upon the weak.
And you'll be subject to the reign of Satan,
and bound to him through sin by cosmic law."

Then Eve and Adam trembled with remorse,
   but Elohim were quick to reassure.
"All is not lost, our dear and treasured children,
   for we've prepared a way for your return.
   Our own Beloved Son, the great Jehovah,
   will overcome the bonds of death and sin.
   And if you choose to follow and obey,
   then you will be reclaimed from Satan's chains
   and, through the Holy Spirit, be made whole.
   Then this great rift will be forever healed
   and with Eternal Life you will be crowned."

In gratitude, the man and woman wept
   and cov'nanted to bind themselves to Christ.

"And now," said Mother God with tender care.
"We'll make a coat of skins for you to wear
   as you embark upon your mortal quest.
   This coat, made from the fleece of that slain lamb,
   will cover and protect you on your way
   as you enrobe yourselves in mem'ry of
   the Lamb of God, who'll give his life for you.

And, I, too, will be with you 'til the end."

Once clothed, the man and woman were sent forth,
   evicted from the nutur'ing womb of God,
   cast out into the lone and dreary world.

Then, in a place known only to Themselves
and in the tender oneness of Their bond
the Mother and the Father undertook
the act of purest selflessness and love
as Mother God laid down Her form *pro tem*
that with Her children She could yet abide.

The weeping Father gathered up the form
of His beloved, soulmate, confidante—
not dead, but in a shadowland of grace—
and placed it gently at the foot of that
great tow'ring Tree which at the Center stood.
And there sprang up wild sprigs of lacelike vines
and sprays of fragrant blossoms, burgeoning—
embracing, sheltering the sacred form
of Mother God until that time foretold,
cocooned in living funerary pyre,
with cherubim and flaming sword to guard
the way. Then, in an exhalation of
suspended animation, El, alone,
sealed off the Garden, reliquary of
the body that would rise again in glory
to restore the Earth to her Edenic state.

And, meanwhile, Eve and Adam undertook
their new beginning in a world replete

with sorrow, disappointment, and despair.
But they discovered beauty there—and joy!
Yes, there was pain, but also pure delight.
By their own sweat, they tilled the ground for food,
but found deep satisfaction in their work.
In agony and moil, Eve brought forth young,
each cherished all the more for what they cost.

With gratitude, they praised the name of God.
And with them, ever, was their Holy Guide—
Her, blessing them with wisdom, grace, and light.

Their children grew, begetting other children,
'til generations lived upon the earth,
bright spirits ever seeking further light
while learning, stumbling, growing, grasping, sharing,
then soaring, falling, rising once again.
All helping, hurting, hoping, oft forgetting,
then turning back and hearkening once more.

And then, at the appointed time, was born
the Son of God, the Savior of the world,
to Mary, valiant maid of Galilee.

With perfect love, He healed the sick and maimed,
and taught great truths to those with ears to hear.
"Please, yoke yourself to me and take my name."

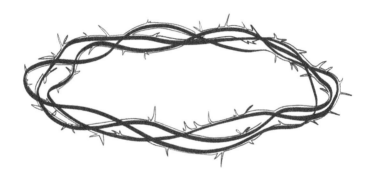

"Come, follow me, and cast on me your sins,
 and I will heal your hearts and give you rest."
"Rejoice." "Fear not." "Forgive." "Judge not." "Love God."
"Have faith. Repent. Be baptized in my name."
"Now, serve." "Do good." "Be kind." and "Feed my sheep."

And when the hour was come, He did not shrink,
but took upon Himself the weight of sin,
of heartbreak, illness, loneliness, and fear,
and, heaving, healed the breach wrought by the Fall.

By means unknowable to human mind,
the Son, half-mortal, faced alone the full
and daunting force of Satan's dreadful might
unclamping evil's deadly choking vise,
then rose—all praise!—to set the captives free
from Satan's coil of sorrow, sin, and death.

His body slain and taken up again,
He soared, the Wingèd One, to Father's side,
but promised first to gift the Holy Ghost
whose light-filled presence hovered ever near
to guide and teach and purify with fire.
And promised, too, that He would come again
when earth was ripe and mortal work was done.
"My peace I leave with you. Remember me."

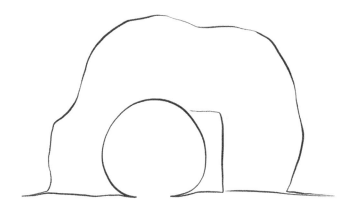

And many generations more were born
into this holy mess of mortal life,
to gain, to lose, to love, to hate, to use
and oft abuse the splendid scope of their
free choice. And as they exercised their will,
they co-created what the world would be.

Receiving light, rejecting light, and then
receiving more, preparing for that day
when Jesus Christ, Redeemer of the World,
will come again in robes resplendent to
reclaim all those He has redeemed. And God
Shaddi Almighty will again take up
Her body and ascend to take Her place
upon the throne. And all who overcame
the world, bearing tribulation, will
be fed, and led to fountains pure and free.
And God will wipe away the tears of all
who suffered grief and pain, injustice, and
abuse—for no more malice will exist:
no fear, no war, nor hunger, nor contempt,
for grace has conquered all, and evil has
no sway. The former things are passed away
and all things are made new: perfected, whole
in Jesus Christ, the Finisher of all.

And then, what songs of jubilation will
ring out throughout the heavens, holy strains
of purest gladness sung by all the heirs
of God—Mother Eve and Father Adam
and all of their descendants throughout time,
now linked and sealed together as a vast,
enduring unit in a plexus ever-
lasting of relationship and joy.

Glory to the Parents, and glory to
the Lamb and to the Dove, and glory, glory
glory to each precious son and daughter
who chooses light, and growth, and hope, and love.

QUESTIONS & TOPICS FOR DISCUSSION

1. Why do you think the author wrote *Brighter and Brighter* as an epic poem rather than, say, a short story or a novel?

2. What makes *Brighter and Brighter* an epic poem? What are the conventions of epic poetry?

3. Is Lucifer/Satan a sympathetic character at any point in the poem? Why or why not?

4. What role does light play in the narrative? What do we learn about light in the hymn sung by the hosts of heaven on pages 12–13?

5. How does the portrayal of Eve differ from Milton's portrayal of Eve in *Paradise Lost?*

6. What theological and moral assumptions underlie *Brighter and Brighter?*

7. What must followers of The Morning Star (Lucifer) give up in exchange for salvation? (see pages 7 and 32)

8. Characterize the relationship between Elohim (Father and Mother) and Lucifer.

9. What does *Brighter and Brighter* have to say about the nature and source of evil?

10. What is meant on page 21 by "a paired redemption"? How is this further clarified on pages 23 and 50?

11. How is Satan's power different from Elohim's power? (see page 32)

12. According to the poem, how will "balance be restored and nature healed"? (see page 28)

13. What is the relationship between the earth and the Garden? (see page 36)

14. According to the poem, what is the forbidden fruit and why does partaking of it require that Adam and Eve leave the Garden? (see pages 36, 38, 42, and 49)

15. Satan, the Father of all Lies, tells Eve that she must partake of the forbidden fruit because "there is no other way" (page 44). Is it possible that there was another way?

16. How does Satan's directive to eat the lamb provide a powerful juxtaposition to Christ's plea to feed His sheep? (see pages 42, 45 and 57).

17. What is the substance of the argument Eve presents to Adam on pages 45–47?

18. In the accounts of the Creation recorded in both Genesis and Moses as well as in the fictionalized *Brighter and Brighter*, only Adam is commanded not to partake of the forbidden fruit. This happens before Eve is formed. (See Genesis 2: 15–24 and Moses 3:15–24.) How does this change things, if at all?

19. Where is the body of Mother God placed? Why is this significant? (see page 52)

20. Discuss the larger themes in the poem—agency, hubris, love, relationship, progression, healing, balance and equality, etc.

21. A cherished Latter-day Saint belief is that we have a Heavenly Mother as well as a Heavenly Father. Does the fictional speculation in *Brighter and Brighter* that Heavenly Mother willingly chose to lay aside her glorified body for a time in order to more fully and powerfully be with Her children during mortality diminish or increase Her importance in your view?

22. What is the definition of kairos (page 9)? Have you experienced a defining moment (or several) in your own life?

23. In what ways can we be "pure conduits of light—receiving light, bequeathing light in one continuous flow"? (page 12)

24. How does a work like *Brighter and Brighter* blur the lines between fiction and nonfiction? What larger purpose might this serve?

25. How does the poem's reimagining of premortal life, the Creation, the Garden, the Fall, and mortality open up new possibilities in your mind?

26. When Elohim (Father and Mother) introduce Adam into the Garden, They give him stewardship over the plants and animals in that realm. Is there a difference between stewardship and ownership? (page 36) How might our relationship to the world around us change if we better understood this difference?

27. Might consent be an eternal principle? (see page 39) How does this play into the concept of agency?

28. In what sense might we, as God's children, be co-creators of "what the world would be"? (page 59)

29. In what sense is *Brighter and Brighter* a theodicy? How does it account for the problem of evil? Discuss the interplay in the poem between the ideas of creation ex materia, eternal laws, agency, evil, light, progression, and love.

30. What is the final vision of immortality and Eternal Life described in the closing stanzas of *Brighter and Brighter*?

ACKNOWLEDGMENTS

As John Donne so famously affirms, no man is an island. Neither is any woman. I freely acknowledge my indebtedness to the writings and influence of countless individuals including but not limited to Origen, Jerome, Epiphanius, Hippolytus, Theophilus, Irenaeos, Melito of Sardis, Aphrahat, Ephrem, Symeon of Mesopotamia, Julian of Norwich, all the Latter-day prophets from Joseph Smith to the present, Eliza R. Snow, Chieko Okasaki, Beverly Campbell, Sheri Dew, Carol Lynn Pearson, Margaret Baker, Catherine Worthington, Mcarthur Krishna, Valerie Hudson, Val Larsen, Neylan McBaine, Rachel Hunt Steenblik, David L. Paulsen, Martin Pulido, J.M. Huntington, Fiona Givens, Terryl Givens, Kathryn Knight

Sonntag, James Glenn, Erica Glenn, Kedric Glenn, Kelli Glenn, Patrick Glenn, Karine Glenn, Dylan Glenn, Rachel Glenn, and Devin Glenn.

Canonized scripture and other works of holy writ were sources of significant inspiration for me. I include the Old Testament (especially Genesis 1–3 and Proverbs 3), the New Testament (especially Revelation 12), the Book of Mormon (especially 1 Nephi 11), the Doctrine and Covenants (especially sections 88 and 93), and the Pearl of Great Price (especially Moses 1–4 and 7) as well as the King Follett Discourse, The Gospel According to the Hebrews, the Pseudo-Clementines, The Shepherd of Hermas, The Gospel of Thomas, The Acts of Thomas, and The Odes of Solomon.

I am also profoundly grateful to J. Kirk Richards for allowing us to use his glorious painting "Creator Goddess" for the cover of *Brighter and Brighter* and to Sara Forbush for her evocative internal illustrations.

Finally, many thanks to the entire team at BCC Press, most especially Michael Austin, cheerleader and editor extraordinaire.

SHARLEE MULLINS GLENN has published poetry, essays, short stories, articles, and criticism in periodicals as varied as *Women's Studies*, *The Southern Literary Journal*, *Segullah*, *BYU Studies Quarterly*, *Ladybug*, and *The New York Times*. She is also an award-winning author of children's books, publishing with G. P. Putnam's Sons, Harcourt, and Abrams, and a contributing editor for *Wayfare*. Sharlee is the recipient of the Dolly Gray Children's Literature Award for *Keeping Up with Roo* (Putnam) and the Norman A. Sugarman Children's Biography Honor Award for *Library on Wheels: Mary Lemist Titcomb and America's First Bookmobile* (Abrams).

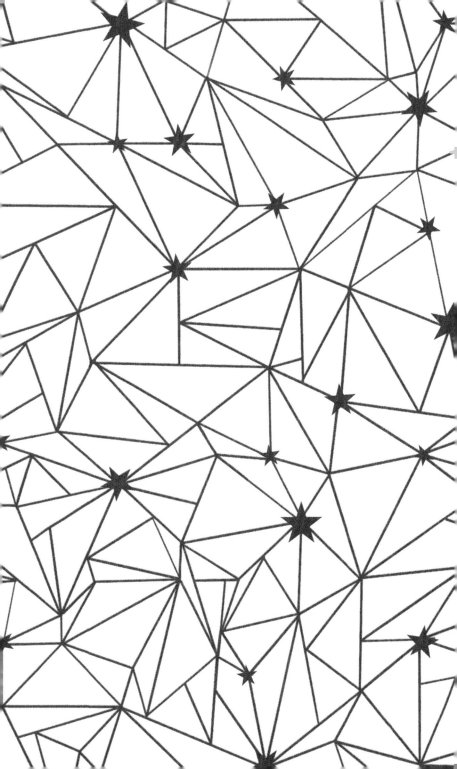

Made in the USA
Monee, IL
03 May 2025

16784384R10056